D
A
Y

6

How does this affect what I believe?

DAY

7

How does this affect what I believe?

_____
_____
_____
_____
_____
_____
_____
_____
_____
_____
_____
_____
_____
_____
_____
_____
_____
_____
_____
_____
_____
_____
_____
_____
_____

D
A
Y

8

How does this affect what I believe?

D
A
Y

9

How does this affect what I believe?

How does this affect what I believe?

D
A
Y

1
1

How does this affect what I believe?

How does this affect what I believe?

DAY 13

How does this affect what I believe?

How does this affect what I believe?

D A Y

1 5

How does this affect what I believe?

How does this affect what I believe?

**D
A
Y**

**1
7**

How does this affect what I believe?

How does this affect what I believe?

**D
A
Y

1
9**

How does this affect what I believe?

How does this affect what I believe?

DAY

21

How does this affect what I believe?

_____
_____
_____
_____
_____
_____
_____
_____
_____
_____
_____
_____
_____
_____
_____
_____
_____
_____
_____
_____
_____
_____
_____
_____

DAY 22

How does this affect what I believe?

DAY

23

How does this affect what I believe?

How does this affect what I believe?

DAY

25

How does this affect what I believe?

How does this affect what I believe?

DAY

27

How does this affect what I believe?

How does this affect what I believe?

**D
A
Y

2
9**

_____

_____

_____

_____

_____

_____

_____

_____

_____

_____

_____

_____

_____

_____

_____

_____

_____

_____

_____

_____

_____

_____

_____

How does this affect what I believe?

_____

_____

_____

_____

_____

_____

_____

_____

_____

_____

_____

_____

_____

_____

_____

_____

_____

_____

_____

_____

_____

_____

_____

_____

DAY 30

How does this affect what I believe?

D
A
Y

3
1

How does this affect what I believe?

_____

_____

_____

_____

_____

_____

_____

_____

_____

_____

_____

_____

_____

_____

_____

_____

_____

_____

_____

_____

_____

_____

_____

DAY

32

How does this affect what I believe?

DAY 33

How does this affect what I believe?

How does this affect what I believe?

**D
A
Y**

**3
5**

How does this affect what I believe?

How does this affect what I believe?

DAY

37

How does this affect what I believe?

_____

_____

_____

_____

_____

_____

_____

_____

_____

_____

_____

_____

_____

_____

_____

_____

_____

_____

_____

_____

_____

_____

D
A
Y

3
8

How does this affect what I believe?

DAY

3
9

How does this affect what I believe?

How does this affect what I believe?

DAY

41

How does this affect what I believe?

How does this affect what I believe?

DAY

43

How does this affect what I believe?

_____
_____
_____
_____
_____
_____
_____
_____
_____
_____
_____
_____
_____
_____
_____
_____
_____
_____
_____
_____
_____
_____

D
A
Y

4
4

How does this affect what I believe?

DAY

45

How does this affect what I believe?

How does this affect what I believe?

DAY

47

How does this affect what I believe?

How does this affect what I believe?

DAY

49

How does this affect what I believe?

_____
_____
_____
_____
_____
_____
_____
_____
_____
_____
_____
_____
_____
_____
_____
_____
_____
_____
_____
_____
_____
_____
_____

DAY

50

How does this affect what I believe?

D
A
Y

5
1

How does this affect what I believe?

How does this affect what I believe?

**D
A
Y

5
3**

How does this affect what I believe?

How does this affect what I believe?

D
A
Y

5
/
5

How does this affect what I believe?

How does this affect what I believe?

**D
A
Y

5
7**

How does this affect what I believe?

DAY

58

How does this affect what I believe?

How does this affect what I believe?

How does this affect what I believe?

DAY

61

How does this affect what I believe?

How does this affect what I believe?

How does this affect what I believe?

_____

_____

_____

_____

_____

_____

_____

_____

_____

_____

_____

_____

_____

_____

_____

_____

_____

_____

_____

_____

_____

D
A
Y

6
4

How does this affect what I believe?

DAY

65

How does this affect what I believe?

How does this affect what I believe?

**D
A
Y

6
7**

How does this affect what I believe?

How does this affect what I believe?

DAY

69

How does this affect what I believe?

How does this affect what I believe?

DAY

71

How does this affect what I believe?

How does this affect what I believe?

D
A
Y

7
3

How does this affect what I believe?

_____

_____

_____

_____

_____

_____

_____

_____

_____

_____

_____

_____

_____

_____

_____

_____

_____

_____

_____

_____

_____

_____

D
A
Y

7
4

How does this affect what I believe?

DAY

75

How does this affect what I believe?

_____
_____
_____
_____
_____
_____
_____
_____
_____
_____
_____
_____
_____
_____
_____
_____
_____
_____
_____
_____
_____
_____

D
A
Y

7
6

How does this affect what I believe?

DAY 77

How does this affect what I believe?

_____

_____

_____

_____

_____

_____

_____

_____

_____

_____

_____

_____

_____

_____

_____

_____

_____

_____

_____

_____

_____

_____

_____

_____

How does this affect what I believe?

DAY

79

How does this affect what I believe?

How does this affect what I believe?

D
A
Y

8
1

How does this affect what I believe?

How does this affect what I believe?

How does this affect what I believe?

How does this affect what I believe?

**D
A
Y**

**8
5**

How does this affect what I believe?

How does this affect what I believe?

DAY

87

_____

_____

_____

_____

_____

_____

_____

_____

_____

_____

_____

_____

_____

_____

_____

_____

_____

_____

_____

_____

_____

_____

_____

How does this affect what I believe?

How does this affect what I believe?

DAY

89

How does this affect what I believe?

How does this affect what I believe?

**D
A
Y**

**9
1**

How does this affect what I believe?

How does this affect what I believe?

How does this affect what I believe?

How does this affect what I believe?

How does this affect what I believe?

How does this affect what I believe?

**D
A
Y**

**9
7**

How does this affect what I believe?

How does this affect what I believe?

DAY 99

How does this affect what I believe?

How does this affect what I believe?

How does this affect what I believe?

How does this affect what I believe?

How does this affect what I believe?

How does this affect what I believe?

DAY 105

How does this affect what I believe?

_____

_____

_____

_____

_____

_____

_____

_____

_____

_____

_____

_____

_____

_____

_____

_____

_____

_____

_____

_____

_____

_____

_____

_____

DAY 106

How does this affect what I believe?

DAY 107

How does this affect what I believe?

How does this affect what I believe?

DAY 109

How does this affect what I believe?

How does this affect what I believe?

DAY

111

How does this affect what I believe?

How does this affect what I believe?

DAY 113

How does this affect what I believe?

How does this affect what I believe?

DAY 115

How does this affect what I believe?

How does this affect what I believe?

DAY

117

How does this affect what I believe?

How does this affect what I believe?

DAY

119

How does this affect what I believe?

How does this affect what I believe?

DAY

121

How does this affect what I believe?

How does this affect what I believe?

**D
A
Y

1
2
3**

How does this affect what I believe?

How does this affect what I believe?

D A Y

1 2 5

How does this affect what I believe?

How does this affect what I believe?

DAY 127

How does this affect what I believe?

How does this affect what I believe?

DAY

129

How does this affect what I believe?

How does this affect what I believe?

How does this affect what I believe?

How does this affect what I believe?

How does this affect what I believe?

How does this affect what I believe?

How does this affect what I believe?

How does this affect what I believe?

DAY

137

How does this affect what I believe?

How does this affect what I believe?

D A Y

1
3
9

_____

_____

_____

_____

_____

_____

_____

_____

_____

_____

_____

_____

_____

_____

_____

_____

_____

_____

_____

_____

_____

_____

_____

_____

How does this affect what I believe?

How does this affect what I believe?

DAY

141

How does this affect what I believe?

How does this affect what I believe?

DAY

143

HOW WE WORSHIP
Part 2: The Celebration of the Christian Mystery

The second section of the *Catechism* presents how we live the truths of the Faith through the "divine service," which is the Liturgy and the sacraments, through which Jesus Christ acts today in the world. In the Liturgy and the sacraments, Jesus renews us and communicates to us the divine life that he came to give us, redeeming us from our sins and making us sharers in the divine nature.

How does this affect how I worship?

DAY

145

How does this affect how I worship?

DAY

146

How does this affect how I worship?

DAY

147

How does this affect how I worship?

How does this affect how I worship?

DAY 149

How does this affect how I worship?

How does this affect how I worship?

DAY

151

_____

_____

_____

_____

_____

_____

_____

_____

_____

_____

_____

_____

_____

_____

_____

_____

_____

_____

_____

_____

_____

_____

_____

_____

_____

How does this affect how I worship?

How does this affect how I worship?

How does this affect how I worship?

How does this affect how I worship?

DAY

155

How does this affect how I worship?

How does this affect how I worship?

How does this affect how I worship?

DAY 158

How does this affect how I worship?

_____
_____
_____
_____
_____
_____
_____
_____
_____
_____
_____
_____
_____
_____
_____
_____
_____
_____
_____
_____
_____
_____
_____
_____
_____
_____

DAY 159

How does this affect how I worship?

How does this affect how I worship?

How does this affect how I worship?

DAY 162

How does this affect how I worship?

DAY 163

_____

_____

_____

_____

_____

_____

_____

_____

_____

_____

_____

_____

_____

_____

_____

_____

_____

_____

_____

_____

_____

_____

How does this affect how I worship?

How does this affect how I worship?

DAY 165

CCC 1210-1222

How does this affect how I worship?

DAY

1
6
6

How does this affect how I worship?

DAY

167

How does this affect how I worship?

_____
_____
_____
_____
_____
_____
_____
_____
_____
_____
_____
_____
_____
_____
_____
_____
_____
_____
_____
_____
_____
_____
_____
_____
_____

DAY 168

How does this affect how I worship?

**D
A
Y

1
6
9**

How does this affect how I worship?

How does this affect how I worship?

DAY

171

How does this affect how I worship?

How does this affect how I worship?

DAY 173

How does this affect how I worship?

How does this affect how I worship?

D
A
Y

1
7
5

How does this affect how I worship?

How does this affect how I worship?

How does this affect how I worship?

How does this affect how I worship?

DAY

179

How does this affect how I worship?

How does this affect how I worship?

DAY 181

How does this affect how I worship?

_____

_____

_____

_____

_____

_____

_____

_____

_____

_____

_____

_____

_____

_____

_____

_____

_____

_____

_____

_____

_____

_____

_____

How does this affect how I worship?

DAY 183

How does this affect how I worship?

_____
_____
_____
_____
_____
_____
_____
_____
_____
_____
_____
_____
_____
_____
_____
_____
_____
_____
_____
_____
_____
_____
_____
_____

DAY

184

How does this affect how I worship?

DAY 185

How does this affect how I worship?

_____
_____
_____
_____
_____
_____
_____
_____
_____
_____
_____
_____
_____
_____
_____
_____
_____
_____
_____
_____
_____
_____

DAY

186

How does this affect how I worship?

D A Y

1 8 7

How does this affect how I worship?

How does this affect how I worship?

How does this affect how I worship?

How does this affect how I worship?

How does this affect how I worship?

How does this affect how I worship?

DAY 193

How does this affect how I worship?

How does this affect how I worship?

How does this affect how I worship?

DAY 196

How does this affect how I worship?

DAY

197

How does this affect how I worship?

_____

_____

_____

_____

_____

_____

_____

_____

_____

_____

_____

_____

_____

_____

_____

_____

_____

_____

_____

_____

_____

_____

_____

How does this affect how I worship?

D
A
Y

1
9
9

How does this affect how I worship?

How does this affect how I worship?

How does this affect how I worship?

DAY 202

How does this affect how I worship?

How does this affect how I worship?

How does this affect how I worship?

D
A
Y

2
0
5

How does this affect how I worship?

How does this affect how I worship?

D
A
Y

2
0
7

How does this affect how I worship?

_____
_____
_____
_____
_____
_____
_____
_____
_____
_____
_____
_____
_____
_____
_____
_____
_____
_____
_____
_____
_____
_____

DAY 208

How does this affect how I worship?

How does this affect how I worship?

How does this affect how I worship?

How does this affect how I worship?

_____

_____

_____

_____

_____

_____

_____

_____

_____

_____

_____

_____

_____

_____

_____

_____

_____

_____

_____

_____

_____

_____

_____

_____

DAY 212

How does this affect how I worship?

DAY 213

How does this affect how I worship?

How does this affect how I worship?

How does this affect how I worship?

How does this affect how I worship?

How does this affect how I worship?

_____
_____
_____
_____
_____
_____
_____
_____
_____
_____
_____
_____
_____
_____
_____
_____
_____
_____
_____
_____
_____
_____
_____
_____

DAY 218

How does this affect how I worship?

How does this affect how I worship?

_____

_____

_____

_____

_____

_____

_____

_____

_____

_____

_____

_____

_____

_____

_____

_____

_____

_____

_____

_____

DAY 220

How does this affect how I worship?

How does this affect how I worship?

How does this affect how I worship?

How does this affect how I worship?

How does this affect how I worship?

DAY 225

How does this affect how I worship?

_____
_____
_____
_____
_____
_____
_____
_____
_____
_____
_____
_____
_____
_____
_____
_____
_____
_____
_____
_____
_____

How does this affect how I worship?

How does this affect how I worship?

How does this affect how I worship?

DAY

229

HOW WE LIVE
Part 3: Life in Christ

Here, the *Catechism* continues to unpack the truths of the Faith and how we live them out. This section, which is dedicated to Christian morality, presents what it means to be "reborn in Christ." We are created for eternal, perfect happiness—which is only found through a real participation in the blessed life that is the Father, Son, and Holy Spirit. The new life we have been given through Baptism requires us to live by the new law of divine love, poured into our hearts through the Spirit (see Romans 5:5).

How can this change the way I live?

How can this change the way I live?

How can this change the way I live?

DAY

233

How can this change the way I live?

How can this change the way I live?

DAY 235

How can this change the way I live?

How can this change the way I live?

DAY

237

How can this change the way I live?

How can this change the way I live?

DAY

239

How can this change the way I live?

How can this change the way I live?

DAY

241

_____
_____
_____
_____
_____
_____
_____
_____
_____
_____
_____
_____
_____
_____
_____
_____
_____
_____
_____
_____
_____
_____
_____
_____
_____

How can this change the way I live?

_____
_____
_____
_____
_____
_____
_____
_____
_____
_____
_____
_____
_____
_____
_____
_____
_____
_____
_____
_____
_____
_____

DAY 242

How can this change the way I live?

DAY

243

How can this change the way I live?

How can this change the way I live?

DAY
245

_____
_____
_____
_____
_____
_____
_____
_____
_____
_____
_____
_____
_____
_____
_____
_____
_____
_____
_____
_____
_____
_____
_____

How can this change the way I live?

_____

_____

_____

_____

_____

_____

_____

_____

_____

_____

_____

_____

_____

_____

_____

_____

_____

_____

_____

_____

_____

DAY 246

How can this change the way I live?

DAY

247

_____

_____

_____

_____

_____

_____

_____

_____

_____

_____

_____

_____

_____

_____

_____

_____

_____

_____

_____

_____

_____

_____

_____

How can this change the way I live?

How can this change the way I live?

How can this change the way I live?

How can this change the way I live?

DAY
251

How can this change the way I live?

How can this change the way I live?

How can this change the way I live?

_____
_____
_____
_____
_____
_____
_____
_____
_____
_____
_____
_____
_____
_____
_____
_____
_____
_____
_____
_____
_____
_____
_____
_____
_____

How can this change the way I live?

D
A
Y

2
5
5

How can this change the way I live?

How can this change the way I live?

DAY 257

How can this change the way I live?

How can this change the way I live?

How can this change the way I live?

How can this change the way I live?

D
A
Y

2
6
1

How can this change the way I live?

How can this change the way I live?

How can this change the way I live?

How can this change the way I live?

DAY 265

How can this change the way I live?

How can this change the way I live?

DAY 267

How can this change the way I live?

_____

_____

_____

_____

_____

_____

_____

_____

_____

_____

_____

_____

_____

_____

_____

_____

_____

_____

_____

_____

_____

_____

_____

_____

DAY

268

How can this change the way I live?

DAY

269

How can this change the way I live?

How can this change the way I live?

DAY

271

How can this change the way I live?

_____
_____
_____
_____
_____
_____
_____
_____
_____
_____
_____
_____
_____
_____
_____
_____
_____
_____
_____
_____
_____
_____
_____

How can this change the way I live?

How can this change the way I live?

How can this change the way I live?

DAY 275

How can this change the way I live?

_____

_____

_____

_____

_____

_____

_____

_____

_____

_____

_____

_____

_____

_____

_____

_____

_____

_____

_____

_____

_____

DAY 276

How can this change the way I live?

DAY

277

_____
_____
_____
_____
_____
_____
_____
_____
_____
_____
_____
_____
_____
_____
_____
_____
_____
_____
_____
_____
_____
_____
_____

How can this change the way I live?

How can this change the way I live?

DAY 279

How can this change the way I live?

How can this change the way I live?

How can this change the way I live?

_____

_____

_____

_____

_____

_____

_____

_____

_____

_____

_____

_____

_____

_____

_____

_____

_____

_____

_____

_____

_____

_____

_____

DAY

282

How can this change the way I live?

**D
A
Y

2
8
3**

How can this change the way I live?

How can this change the way I live?

DAY 285

How can this change the way I live?

How can this change the way I live?

DAY 287

_____
_____
_____
_____
_____
_____
_____
_____
_____
_____
_____
_____
_____
_____
_____
_____
_____
_____
_____
_____
_____
_____
_____
_____

How can this change the way I live?

DAY 288

How can this change the way I live?

DAY

289

How can this change the way I live?

_____

_____

_____

_____

_____

_____

_____

_____

_____

_____

_____

_____

_____

_____

_____

_____

_____

_____

_____

_____

_____

_____

_____

_____

_____

DAY 290

How can this change the way I live?

DAY 291

How can this change the way I live?

How can this change the way I live?

DAY 293

How can this change the way I live?

_____
_____
_____
_____
_____
_____
_____
_____
_____
_____
_____
_____
_____
_____
_____
_____
_____
_____
_____
_____
_____
_____
_____
_____

DAY 294

How can this change the way I live?

DAY
295

How can this change the way I live?

How can this change the way I live?

DAY 297

How can this change the way I live?

How can this change the way I live?

DAY 299

How can this change the way I live?

How can this change the way I live?

DAY

301

How can this change the way I live?

How can this change the way I live?

How can this change the way I live?

_____
_____
_____
_____
_____
_____
_____
_____
_____
_____
_____
_____
_____
_____
_____
_____
_____
_____
_____
_____
_____
_____
_____

DAY 304

How can this change the way I live?

DAY

305

_____

_____

_____

_____

_____

_____

_____

_____

_____

_____

_____

_____

_____

_____

_____

_____

_____

_____

_____

_____

_____

_____

_____

_____

_____

How can this change the way I live?

How can this change the way I live?

DAY 307

How can this change the way I live?

How can this change the way I live?

DAY

309

How can this change the way I live?

How can this change the way I live?

DAY 311

How can this change the way I live?

How can this change the way I live?

DAY

313

How can this change the way I live?

How can this change the way I live?

DAY 315

How can this change the way I live?

How can this change the way I live?

How can this change the way I live?

How can this change the way I live?

How can this change the way I live?

How can this change the way I live?

DAY

3
2
1

How can this change the way I live?

How can this change the way I live?

How can this change the way I live?

How can this change the way I live?

How can this change the way I live?

How can this change the way I live?

DAY

327

HOW WE PRAY
Part 4: Christian Prayer

The final section brings our journey through the *Catechism* to a fitting close. Since we live the very life of God through grace as a result of our baptism, there is only one appropriate response to this incredible gift—prayer. Through prayer, we turn to God to more closely live out his life in us and grow more deeply in our relationship with him.

How might this change the way I pray?

_____
_____
_____
_____
_____
_____
_____
_____
_____
_____
_____
_____
_____
_____
_____
_____
_____
_____
_____
_____
_____
_____
_____

How might this change the way I pray?

How might this change the way I pray?

DAY

331

_____
_____
_____
_____
_____
_____
_____
_____
_____
_____
_____
_____
_____
_____
_____
_____
_____
_____
_____
_____
_____
_____
_____
_____
_____

How might this change the way I pray?

How might this change the way I pray?

**D
A
Y**

**3
3
3**

How might this change the way I pray?

How might this change the way I pray?

DAY

3
3
5

How might this change the way I pray?

How might this change the way I pray?

How might this change the way I pray?

_____

_____

_____

_____

_____

_____

_____

_____

_____

_____

_____

_____

_____

_____

_____

_____

_____

_____

_____

_____

_____

DAY

338

How might this change the way I pray?

_____
_____
_____
_____
_____
_____
_____
_____
_____
_____
_____
_____
_____
_____
_____
_____
_____
_____
_____
_____
_____
_____
_____
_____
_____

DAY

339

How might this change the way I pray?

How might this change the way I pray?

DAY

341

How might this change the way I pray?

_____

_____

_____

_____

_____

_____

_____

_____

_____

_____

_____

_____

_____

_____

_____

_____

_____

_____

_____

_____

_____

_____

_____

_____

How might this change the way I pray?

D
A
Y

3
4
3

_____

_____

_____

_____

_____

_____

_____

_____

_____

_____

_____

_____

_____

_____

_____

_____

_____

_____

_____

_____

_____

_____

_____

How might this change the way I pray?

_____

_____

_____

_____

_____

_____

_____

_____

_____

_____

_____

_____

_____

_____

_____

_____

_____

_____

_____

_____

_____

_____

_____

_____

DAY

344

How might this change the way I pray?

How might this change the way I pray?

How might this change the way I pray?

DAY

347

_____
_____
_____
_____
_____
_____
_____
_____
_____
_____
_____
_____
_____
_____
_____
_____
_____
_____
_____
_____
_____
_____

How might this change the way I pray?

How might this change the way I pray?

How might this change the way I pray?

How might this change the way I pray?

How might this change the way I pray?

How might this change the way I pray?

DAY

353

How might this change the way I pray?

_____

_____

_____

_____

_____

_____

_____

_____

_____

_____

_____

_____

_____

_____

_____

_____

_____

_____

_____

_____

_____

_____

D
A
Y

3
5
4

How might this change the way I pray?

DAY

355

How might this change the way I pray?

How might this change the way I pray?

How might this change the way I pray?

_____

_____

_____

_____

_____

_____

_____

_____

_____

_____

_____

_____

_____

_____

_____

_____

_____

_____

_____

_____

_____

DAY 358

How might this change the way I pray?

DAY

359

How might this change the way I pray?

How might this change the way I pray?

How might this change the way I pray?

DAY 362

How might this change the way I pray?

DAY

363

CCC 2846-2856

How might this change the way I pray?

_____
_____
_____
_____
_____
_____
_____
_____
_____
_____
_____
_____
_____
_____
_____
_____
_____
_____
_____
_____
_____
_____

How might this change the way I pray?

_____

_____

_____

_____

_____

_____

_____

_____

_____

_____

_____

_____

_____

_____

_____

_____

_____

_____

_____

_____

_____

_____

_____

_____

D
A
Y

3
6
5

Congratulations!
You have completed
The Catechism in a Year!

Get the **Catechism used** by Fr. Mike Schmitz **in *The Catechism in a Year*** Podcast!

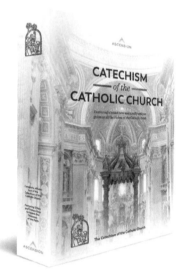

With the **Catechism of the Catholic Church**, **Ascension Edition**, Catholics will encounter the truth and beauty of the Catholic Faith organized to help them learn how to love their faith fully, defend it intelligently, and celebrate it in their daily lives.

The **Ascension Edition** features the exclusive **Foundations of Faith** approach to understanding Catholic teaching. This built-in guide makes it easy to see how the *Catechism* provides Catholics with a blueprint for learning how to better know, love, and serve God that incorporates both Sacred Scripture and Tradition.

Prepare to understand the *Catechism* and the Catholic Faith like never before!